The Perfect Wedding

I Talk You Talk Press

CONTENTS

I Talk You Talk Press

CHAPTER ONE

It's Friday night. Treena and Stan are walking beside the sea. It's raining and it's cold. They can hear the waves crashing against the seawall.

"I'd like to go to the pub," says Stan.

"We don't have any money," says Treena.

"We never have any money!" says Stan.

Treena doesn't say anything. Treena has a job. She works in a supermarket. Stan doesn't have a job. Sometimes he finds a job, but he soon quits. He says, "the boss doesn't like me." Or, "the company didn't pay me enough money."

Treena lives with her sister, Sharon, in a one-bedroom apartment. Treena and Sharon's parents died in a car accident when Treena was 12 and Sharon was 10 years old. They lived with their grandmother. When Treena finished high school, she got a job and an apartment. When Sharon left high school, she went to the local community college. She is studying to be a makeup artist. The government pays her fees, and they give Sharon a little money to live on, but Sharon spends her money on clothes and having a good time. She lives in Treena's apartment. Treena pays for everything. Sharon is very selfish.

Stan is Treena's boyfriend. He lives with his family. Treena has never met them. Stan was born in Poland, but his family moved to England when he was eight years old. He has two sisters. Stan says the house is very small. About six months ago, Stan's father went to Poland. His mother, Stan's grandmother, came back to England with him. There are three bedrooms in his family's house. His parents have one bedroom. His sisters have a bedroom. His grandmother has

Stan's bedroom. So Stan sleeps in the living room. He hates it.

Stan is often bad-tempered. He doesn't like his life. Treena wants Stan to get a job. Stan is very clever, and she wants him to try harder. She doesn't say anything to Stan about it because she loves him very much. But Stan never says he loves Treena.

"I want to go home, Stan," says Treena. "It's so cold, and I'm tired. I have to work tomorrow."

"OK," says Stan. "I will go to see my friend Jaz tomorrow morning. He has bought a motorbike! Then I will watch soccer with my friends. If you have some money, maybe we can go to the pub tomorrow night. Why don't you call me?"

"OK," says Treena.

CHAPTER TWO

Treena works at the supermarket on Saturday mornings. This Saturday, when she finishes work at 12:30pm, she takes her coat and bag from the staff room and walks out of the back door of the supermarket. She plans to clean her apartment and do her laundry.

I am sure Sharon's laundry will be there too, she thinks. *Sharon should wash her own clothes. But if I don't wash Sharon's clothes, she will take my clothes. When the laundry is finished, I will go to visit my grandmother.*

In the street behind the supermarket, Treena sees Stan. He is waiting for her. She is very surprised.

"Treena! Treena!" he shouts. "Let's get married."

"What?" Treena is shocked.

"I have some wonderful news!" says Stan. "But we have to get married."

Treena laughs. "I am in my work uniform, and we are standing in the street. And you are asking me to marry you."

"Yes," says Stan, laughing. He is very cheerful. "I am asking you to marry me."

Treena is happy. *Stan must love me,* she thinks.

Stan takes Treena's hand and takes her into a cafe. They sit down, and Stan orders two coffees.

"I went to see my friend Jaz this morning. He lives with his uncle. Jaz has a new job. He will leave this town and go to live in Liverpool. But he is worried about his uncle. When he goes to Liverpool, his uncle will be alone in the house. His uncle's eyes are very bad, He is almost blind.

"The house is very big. It has an apartment upstairs. I went with Jaz to talk to his uncle. His uncle says we can have the apartment. The rent is very low because we will help Jaz's uncle. His name is Jeremy Bilton. He needs help with letters, and supermarket shopping, and things like that. But he is very old fashioned. He said, 'You can live here if you are married, but you cannot live here if you are not married.' So I told him that we planned to get married. He is happy. And we can move in very soon!"

Treena wants to cry. Stan doesn't love her. He only wants to leave home. He only wants to get married so that they can get the apartment.

"Well," says Stan. "Shall we take the apartment? When can we get married?"

Treena doesn't say anything.

I love Stan very much but Stan does not love me, she thinks. *If I say 'no', I might lose Stan.*

"Yes, Stan," she says. "Let's get married."

Stan leans across the table and kisses Treena.

"How soon can we get married?" he asks.

"I don't know," says Treena. "We have to plan a wedding."

Stan looks surprised. "A wedding? Why don't we go to the town hall and get married? We can have some drinks at the pub with my friends afterwards."

"No, Stan. We are going to have a proper wedding. It will be a very small wedding and it will have to be cheap. But we will get married in a church with our families, and we will have a party afterwards."

Treena feels strongly about this. *Maybe Stan doesn't love me, but we will have a proper wedding.*

Stan thinks about it. *My parents don't know about Treena. Maybe they will be angry when I tell them I am getting married. But they will be happier if we have a wedding in a church.*

"Yes, OK. If you want a wedding in church, you can arrange one. But we must get married soon," he says.

"Six weeks?" asks Treena.

"That's too long," says Stan. "Why don't we get married next month? Four weeks."

Treena pays for the coffees and they leave the café.

Stan looks at the time on his phone. "I have to go. I have to meet the guys. We are going to watch a soccer match. Then we are having a goodbye party for Jaz."

They walk into the town. Stan's friends are waiting for him. Stan smiles at Treena.

"I'll call you tomorrow." Stan walks away with his friends. They are shouting and laughing.

CHAPTER THREE

Treena walks back to her apartment. Sharon is not there. It's cold in the apartment. She is very worried and unhappy. *I'm going to get married. I love Stan. I should be happy. But I'm not.*

She lies on her bed with her coat on and cries.

What have I done? I'm going to marry a man who doesn't love me. He only wants to marry me so he can leave home.

After a while, Treena gets up. She cleans the apartment and takes all the laundry to the launderette. The launderette has a small sitting area with piles of newspapers and magazines. While she is waiting for the clothes to wash and dry, she reads magazines. There are some bridal magazines. Treena looks at the dresses.

They are very beautiful. I would love to buy one of those dresses, she thinks.

When the laundry is finished, Treena carries it back to her apartment. There is a note from Sharon.

---*I came back, but you weren't here. I am staying with my friend Lisa tonight. She is having a party.*---

Treena calls her grandmother, but there is no reply. Then Treena remembers. *The old people's club were going on a trip today. My grandmother has gone to visit some gardens. She won't come back until late tonight.*

Treena feels very strange. *I am getting married, and I have no one to tell.*

She heats some soup and makes toast. After she has eaten, she feels better.

I am going to have the perfect wedding, she thinks. *I only have four weeks, but I can do everything. I will find a way to have a very cheap, but perfect wedding.*

She washes the dishes and makes a coffee. She sits in the tiny living room with a pen and a notebook and makes a list.

Treena writes '...church, priest, party, dresses, flowers, invitations...'

I will have a bridesmaid, she thinks. *I guess Sharon will be my bridesmaid. She will need a dress too.*

Treena looks at the list.

This will cost a lot of money, she thinks.

Treena has saved a little money. She has 2000 pounds in the bank.

I will use that money to pay for my wedding. It is not very much but it is all the money I have.

Treena feels tired, so she goes to bed. There is no space in her bedroom because Sharon sleeps there too. Treena cleaned the bedroom before she went to the launderette, but now Sharon's clothes and makeup are everywhere. Usually Treena tidies everything before she goes to bed. But not tonight. She picks up the clothes from the floor and throws them on Sharon's bed. Then she gets into her own bed and falls asleep.

CHAPTER FOUR

The next morning, Treena gets up early. She sends a text to Stan. She writes

---What is the name of your family's church? Who is the priest?---

Stan stays in bed until the afternoon on Sundays.

He won't answer my text until later, she thinks.

She is surprised when she gets an answer very quickly.

---It's St Stephens. The priest's name is Simpson but we call him Father Peter. I am busy today but I will call you tonight.---

Treena calls Father Peter and leaves a message on his answer phone.

She says, "Father Peter. My name is Treena Brown. I'd like to come and talk to you about a wedding in four weeks' time. I'll call you again." Treena says her telephone number. Then she goes out to the supermarket to buy food for the next week.

She finishes putting the food away, and then makes a cup of coffee and a sandwich. She sits at the kitchen table and thinks about her mother and father.

I wish they were alive. I wonder what their wedding was like?

Then Treena remembers a photograph of her parents' wedding. She goes to the living room and finds the box of old photographs. She takes out the wedding photograph and looks at it.

They look so happy, she thinks. *And my mother looks beautiful. Her dress is wonderful. I wonder what happened to her wedding dress. Maybe my grandmother knows. I will ask her.*

Treena goes to see her grandmother. She takes some cookies and a packet of her grandmother's favourite tea. Treena's grandmother lives in a tiny council apartment.

Treena climbs the stairs of the tall apartment building and knocks on her grandmother's door. She has to wait a long time until the door opens. Her grandmother is very old and does everything very slowly.

"Treena! It's nice to see you! Come in!"

Treena goes into the apartment. It is filled with furniture. When Treena's grandmother, moved out of her house, she tried to take all her memories and treasures with her. "Shall I make some tea, Grandma?" asks Treena.

"Yes, that would be nice," answers her grandmother.

Treena makes tea and puts some of the cookies on a plate.

They sit down at the kitchen table.

"How was your trip, Grandma?" asks Treena.

"It was very nice. We went to see Parcevall Hall Gardens. We had a cup of tea in Leeds on the way there. Then we had lunch in the tearooms at the Gardens. On the way back, the bus stopped in Doncaster and we had fish and chips."

Treena laughs. "Grandma, that is all about food! Did you like the gardens?"

Treena's grandmother laughs too. "Oh, the gardens were beautiful! Now, tell me your news," says Grandma. "What did you do this week?"

"Oh, Grandma! Stan asked me to marry him! We will get married in four weeks!" says Treena.

Treena's grandmother looks at Treena. "Why are you getting married?" she asks. "Are you going to have a baby?"

"Oh, no!" Treena is shocked.

"So why are you getting married so quickly?" asks Treena's grandmother.

Treena explains about the apartment.

"I understand," says Treena's grandmother. "Are you happy?"

Am I happy? Treena thinks. *No. I am not happy, but I will not tell my grandmother.*

"Yes, Grandma. I am very happy."

Her grandmother smiles. "That's good. Now tell me about the wedding."

"I haven't planned the wedding yet," says Treena. "It will be very small. I don't have very much money to pay for a wedding. Grandma, what happened to my mother's wedding dress?"

"I don't know. I guess it got lost. Did you want to wear it?"

"Yes, I did," says Treena. "And a new wedding dress will be very expensive."

"I'm sorry Treena. You will have to buy a new one for yourself."

Treena's grandmother stands up. She walks to a bookcase in her living room. She opens a small box and takes out some money.

"Here, Treena. Here is two hundred pounds. It's a present. Use it to buy a dress for yourself."

"Oh, thank you Grandma! You are so kind!"

"I am sorry I don't have much money to give you," says her grandmother.

Treena kisses her grandmother. "This is a lot of money. I am sure I can find a beautiful dress to wear!"

Treena goes home. Sharon is watching television.

"Hi Treena," she says. "What are you cooking for dinner? I'm very hungry."

Treena makes an omelette and a salad. Sharon comes to the kitchen and sits down to eat.

"I have something to tell you," says Treena. "Stan and I are getting married next month. I hope you will be my bridesmaid."

Sharon stops eating and looks at Treena. "Where are you going to live?"

"Stan has found an apartment on the second floor of a big house. The rent is low because we will help the man who owns the house. He cannot see very well."

"Where will I live?" asks Sharon. Her face is red and she looks very angry.

"You can stay here," says Treena. "You get some money from the government for living, and if you get a part-time job, you will have enough money for the rent and food."

Sharon stands up and throws her plate on the floor. She picks up her bag and her jacket. "I hate you!" she shouts. "I'm going to Lisa's house."

Sharon goes out of the apartment and shuts the door very loudly. Treena hears Sharon running down the stairs.

Treena is not hungry any more. She throws the salad and omelette in the garbage bin. She picks up the broken plate and cleans the floor. Then she cleans the kitchen and goes to bed. But she cannot sleep.

Why is Sharon so angry? she thinks. *Why isn't she happy? She always says this apartment is too small for two people. She always says she wants to live alone.*

Finally Treena falls asleep.

CHAPTER FIVE

The next morning when Treena wakes up she is cold and hungry. It is late. She will be late for work. Treena hurries. She doesn't have breakfast. She runs to work, but she is late. Her boss is angry. It is a very bad start to the day.

At lunchtime, Treena goes to the park with her friend Gloria.

She tells Gloria, "Stan asked me to marry him on Saturday."

"Of course you said 'no' "says Gloria.

"I said yes."

"Are you crazy?" Gloria is angry with her friend. "He has no job. He has no money. He likes to spend time with his friends. He is like a child!"

"But Gloria," says Treena. "I love him."

Gloria thinks it's a very bad idea, but Treena is her friend.

If Treena really loves Stan and he wants to marry her, then I should be happy for her. I only hope Stan loves her, she thinks.

"I'm sorry, Treena," Gloria says. She smiles and hugs her friend. "That was not a nice thing for me to say. If you are happy, then I am happy for you. When are you getting married?"

"Stan wants to get married in four weeks. We can get a cheap apartment. It's in a big house. But we must move into the apartment very soon."

"Tell me about your wedding plans," says Gloria.

"Oh, Gloria. It's very difficult. I have two thousand pounds to pay for everything. And my grandmother gave me two hundred pounds to buy a dress. But it's not enough money."

"No, it's not," says Gloria. "Most wedding dresses cost more than two thousand pounds. And weddings cost about fifteen thousand pounds!"

"What can I do?" asks Treena.

"I will help you," says Gloria. "I am sure you can have a nice wedding for two thousand pounds. I have a good idea about a dress!"

"What's that?" asks Treena.

"When my cousin got married, she bought her dress on the Internet from China. It was very cheap and it looked great! After work we will go to an Internet café and look for wedding dresses."

Treena and Gloria have a good time at the Internet café. There are hundreds of dresses to look at on the Internet. Treena is surprised. Many are very cheap. She is happy because she can buy a dress using the money from her grandmother.

"If I buy one of the cheaper ones, I will have enough money to buy a bridesmaid's dress for Sharon too!" she says.

Then Treena remembers that Sharon is very angry.

Maybe if she has a new dress, she will be happier, she thinks.

Gloria helps Treena choose a dress. They choose a dress for Sharon too. The dresses will arrive in eight days! Treena is very excited and happy.

CHAPTER SIX

When Treena gets back to her apartment, the telephone rings. It is the secretary from the church.

"Father Peter is away until next Monday," she says. "But I can ask some questions now. Please give me your name and the name of the groom."

"Stanislaw Kowalski and Treena Margaret Brown," says Treena.

"Stan Kowalski?" asks the secretary. She sounds very surprised.

"Yes. That's right," says Treena.

"When do you plan to get married?" asks the secretary.

"On November fifteenth," says Treena.

"That is very soon. It might be difficult," says the secretary. "Why are you getting married so soon? Are you going to have a baby?"

"No," says Treena. "My grandmother asked the same question. We have a chance to get a very cheap apartment, but we must move into the apartment in November."

"OK," says the secretary. "I will try. Usually Father Peter says you must plan three months or more ahead. But he knows the Kowalski family well. They are a very good family. So maybe he will say it is OK. Come with Stan on Tuesday next week. Can you come at five thirty pm?"

"Yes," says Treena. "That's OK. Thank you."

Treena sends a text message to Stan. She tells him about the meeting at the church. She asks him to make a list of guests. She wants to know how many people will come. She wants to send invitations.

Stan sends back an answer. It says, ---*OK.*---

Treena has a very busy week. Gloria helps her a lot. They find a pub near the church that will serve sandwiches, tea and coffee plus one glass of champagne for each guest for ten pounds per person.

"If anyone wants to drink more alcohol, they can go to the bar and buy their own," says Gloria.

Gloria's mother worked in a flower shop when she was young. She can arrange flowers very well. She will prepare flowers for Sharon and Treena to carry, flowers for the church and flowers for the party in the pub.

Gloria's mother says, "Gloria will buy the flowers from the market. I will arrange them for you. It will be our wedding present to you!"

Treena knows that she is lucky to have such a good friend.

Treena doesn't see Stan all week. He doesn't call her. He doesn't send any text messages. This is very strange, but she is busy, so she doesn't worry about it. Sharon doesn't come back to the apartment. She stays with her friend Lisa. Treena tries to call her, but Sharon will not talk to her. Treena is unhappy because Sharon is angry. On Saturday, Stan sends a message to Treena.

---*Busy all weekend.*---

He's watching soccer with his friends, thinks Treena.

On Sunday Treena goes to visit her grandmother. She tells her grandmother about the plans for the wedding. She tells her grandmother about the dress.

"It will arrive on Tuesday or Wednesday!" she says. "I'm so excited!"

CHAPTER SEVEN

Treena sends a text to Stan on Monday night.

---*Don't forget. Meeting with Father Peter – be at the church at 5:30pm!*---

At work in the supermarket, Treena gets a phone call from the post office. A parcel is waiting for her. It's too big for the mailbox. She has to pick it up from the post office.

"It's the dresses!" Treena tells Gloria. "The dresses are here!"

Gloria goes and talks to the boss. "It's a very rainy day and we are not so busy," she says. "Treena has important things to do. Please let her leave early today."

The boss says, "OK."

Treena leaves work at 4:00pm. She goes to the post office to pick up the parcel. She takes a big plastic bag from work to put the parcel in. She doesn't want the dresses to get wet. She puts the parcel in the plastic bag and hurries home to her apartment.

She takes the parcel out of the plastic bag and unwraps it very carefully. She lays her wedding dress on the bed. It is beautiful!

She takes the dress for Sharon out of the box too. It is bright red and very pretty. Treena thinks Sharon will love it.

She puts Sharon's dress on a hanger and hides it in the clothes wardrobe.

She puts the wedding dress on a hanger too. It is too big for the wardrobe so she hangs it on the bedroom door. Treena sits on the bed and looks at the dress. She feels very happy about the wedding.

I am so lucky, she thinks. *I love Stan and I am going to marry him. I have a beautiful dress to wear. It will be the perfect wedding.*

Treena looks at her mobile phone. It is 5:15 pm.

I have no time to try on the dress now, she thinks. *I must leave now or I will be late for the meeting with Father Peter.*

She finds a big bed sheet and carefully covers the dress. Then she takes her bag, her raincoat and her umbrella and leaves.

Treena hurries to St Stephen's Church. Father Peter is waiting for her. He is very nice. He makes coffee and they sit in a small meeting room to wait for Stan.

"Usually it is not possible to get married so quickly. But you are marrying a Kowalski. They are a good family and I know them well," he says. "You must go to the town hall and fill in some papers. But I can do everything else for you."

At 5:45 pm, Father Peter and Treena are still waiting for Stan. Treena tries to call him, but his phone is turned off.

"I'm sorry, Father Peter," says Treena. "I don't know what has happened."

Father Peter is kind. He says, "I have known Stan since his family came here from Poland. He is a good boy and very clever. But he is very young."

"I don't understand," says Treena.

"Are you sure Stan wants to get married?" asks Father Peter. "Maybe he has changed his mind."

"No! No!" says Treena. "I think he has forgotten this meeting, but I am sure he wants to get married."

"OK," says Father Peter. "I am sorry. I have to go to another meeting now. But here are the papers for arranging the wedding. I know all about Stan so I have written his name, address, date of birth and telephone number on the papers. Please take the papers and write all the information about yourself. Please ask Stan to call me. I want to talk to him."

Treena gets up and shakes hands with Father Peter. She hurries out of the church. Outside it is windy, cold and wet. She puts the papers from Father Peter in her raincoat pocket and starts to walk back to her apartment.

Why didn't Stan come? Why didn't he answer his phone? I was so happy this afternoon but now I am worried again!

Treena is very wet when she arrives at her apartment. She climbs the stairs. The door of the apartment is unlocked. She walks in and hears voices.

Good! Sharon has come back! I will show her the beautiful dress I bought for her. She will be happy.

Treena drops her bag and umbrella inside the door. The voices are coming from the bedroom. Sharon is laughing. Treena hurries to the bedroom and then she stops. She cannot believe it! Lisa and Sharon are lying on Treena's bed. Lisa is wearing the wedding dress! She is painting her fingernails.

"What!" shouts Treena. Lisa and Sharon are surprised. They turn around and Lisa drops the nail polish on the wedding dress. Treena, Sharon and Lisa see the red nail polish run out all over the beautiful white dress.

Treena runs to the door of the apartment. She forgets to take her bag and her umbrella. She runs down the stairs. Her eyes are filled with tears. She cannot see well. She runs across the street in front of a bus. The bus driver tries to stop. He slows down, but the bus hits Treena. She falls to the side of the road. She doesn't move. Someone calls the police and an ambulance. The ambulance takes Treena to hospital. The bus driver is very shocked. A policeman tells the bus driver, "It's OK. She is very lucky. She will be OK. Everyone saw what happened. She ran onto the road in front of your bus. It was not your fault."

CHAPTER EIGHT

Early next morning, Treena is lying in a hospital bed. It hurts when she moves her arms and legs. She has a terrible headache. She can't stop crying. She doesn't want to talk to anyone.

"How is our mystery woman?" asks the doctor.

"She is OK. She was very lucky. She must stay here for two more days. But we don't know who she is," says a nurse. "She will not talk. She cries all the time. We found some papers for a wedding in her pocket. The name on the papers is Kowalski. There was an address and telephone number too. The police called the number last night. Maybe the Kowalskis will know who she is."

Treena closes her eyes. *I want to be alone,* she thinks. *I don't want to talk.*

Just then, two women walk into Treena's hospital room. There is a lot of noise.

Treena opens her eyes. One of the women is young. She looks like Stan. She is tall and slim and blonde. The other woman is older. She has dark hair.

The two women come and sit next to Treena's bed.

"Hi," says the young blonde woman. "I'm Helena. I'm Stan's sister. This is my mother. She doesn't speak English well, so I will translate. We were surprised when a policewoman called us. The police found marriage papers in your pocket. The groom's name is Stanislaw Kowalski. But the space for the bride's name is empty. What's your name? Are you and Stan getting married?"

"I'm Treena Brown," says Treena. "Stan and I were planning a

wedding, but now I don't know. Everything has gone wrong!"
Treena starts crying again.

Helena speaks to her mother in Polish.

Mrs Kowalski asks a question.

"My mother asks what is wrong?" says Helena.

Treena can't talk. She is crying too much.

Mrs Kowalski takes Treena's hands and starts talking. She talks for a long time. Treena doesn't understand anything, but she feels very safe. She feels the woman is very kind. Finally she stops crying.

When Stan's mother stops talking, Helena speaks. "My mother is very confused. Stan did not tell her about you. She is worried because you are very unhappy. She wants to help you. But she doesn't know what to do. Can you please tell us what is wrong?"

Treena starts talking. She tells Mrs Kowalski and Helena that she is Stan's girlfriend. She tells them about the apartment in Mr Bilton's house.

"Stan wanted to get married so that we could have the apartment," says Treena.

Helena translates Treena's words into Polish. Mrs Kowalski looks very angry. She says something and Helena explains.

"My mother is angry. She says that it is a very bad thing. Stan cannot get married when he has no job. He cannot look after a wife. My mother thinks your parents should stop you getting married."

"I don't have any parents. They died a long time ago. I have a sister, but she is younger than me. I have a grandmother, but she is old now," says Treena.

Helena translates and Mrs Kowalski nods her head.

"My mother understands," says Helena. "But I think she is still angry with Stan. She will want to talk to him."

"Where is Stan?" asks Treena.

"We don't know," says Helena. "He went away about ten days ago with one of his friends. Of course, we tried to call him when the policewoman told us about you, but his phone is switched off."

"I think your mother should stop worrying about this wedding," says Treena. "There will be no wedding. Stan didn't come to the meeting with Father Peter. I haven't seen him since the day he asked me to marry him. I don't think he wants to get married."

Helena looks at Treena. "Please tell me. Do you think Stan wants to leave home? Do you think he wants to marry you because he wants his own apartment?"

"Yes," says Treena. "I think so."

"Stan is my brother, and sometimes he is crazy. But he is not a bad person. He asked you to marry him. So, I think he loves you," says Helena.

"But he never says he loves me!" Treena starts crying again.

Mrs Kowalski says something and Helena translates. "My mother heard you say Father Peter. She wants to know about the plans for the wedding."

Treena explains about the church, the party and the flowers. She explains about Sharon. She says, "My sister will not talk to me. She is very angry that I am getting married." Then she says "And now I have no wedding dress! My grandmother gave me the money to buy it and it is covered in red nail polish!"

When Mrs Kowalski hears about the wedding plans, she asks a question.

"Do you love Stan?" asks Helena.

"Of course I do!" answers Treena.

Mrs Kowalski smiles and hugs Treena. Then she stands up. She speaks to Helena.

"My mother says everything will be OK. You must rest and get well. She will come back soon to see you. You must not worry!"

Mrs Kowalski and Helena leave. Treena lies back in her bed. She feels better. The nurse comes in, and Treena gives the nurse her name and address. Then she falls asleep.

CHAPTER NINE

When Treena wakes up, she is very surprised. Stan is sitting next to her bed. He is holding her hand. He looks very tired.

"Stan!" says Treena.

"Oh Treena," says Stan. "I was very frightened when I heard you had an accident and were in hospital. Are you OK?"

"Yes. I'm OK. I can go home tomorrow. I can go back to work next Monday."

"My mother says you can't go home alone. Helena and my other sister, Karolina will stay in your apartment. She says that you will come and stay in their room in our house for a few days. She wants to look after you."

"Your mother is very kind," says Treena. "But it is OK. I will be fine. There won't be a wedding, so I guess she won't see me again."

"What do you mean?" asks Stan. He is very shocked.

"I made a mistake. I love you and I want to marry you. But you don't love me. It is a bad thing to marry when you don't love someone."

"Of course I love you!" shouts Stan.

"But you didn't tell me!" Treena shouts back.

Stan speaks quietly. "I always loved you. I wanted to marry you. But I had no job and we had nowhere to live. As soon as I found Jaz's uncle's apartment I asked you to marry me."

"But why didn't you come to the meeting with Father Peter?"

"I was working in Manchester. I took a day off work and caught the bus. I was coming to the meeting with Father Peter. But the bus broke down on the motorway. I forgot to charge my mobile phone so I couldn't call you. It took a long time to fix the bus and I was very tired. So I went back to Manchester."

"You are working in Manchester?"

"Yes. We are going to get married, so I asked all my friends about getting a job. Culley knew about jobs in Manchester. He was planning to go to Manchester on Sunday, so I went with him. We got a job with a building company there."

"Why didn't you tell me?" asks Treena.

"I wanted to surprise you. I worked for a very long time every day, and I got a lot of money. I wanted to buy you this."

Stan puts his hand in his pocket. He brings out small dark blue box and gives it to Treena. Treena opens the box. Inside is a gold ring with three tiny diamonds.

"I love you, Treena," says Stan.

CHAPTER TEN

Stan is in Manchester. He has a job for two more weeks. Then he will start a new job near to Mr Bilton's house. Treena is staying with the Kowalski family. Treena likes them all very much.

She is happy. Stan loves her. The wedding will be on November 15th. It will be a very big wedding. The Kowalski family have many friends. But Treena doesn't have to worry about the party. Mrs Kowalski and her friends will cook everything. The party will be in the big meeting room next to the church.

Treena worries about her wedding dress and she worries about Sharon. She talks to Helena and Karolina about her.

Helena says that she will go to the college and find Sharon. She will talk to her.

The next day Helena comes to eat dinner with her family and Treena.

"I found Sharon. I talked to her," says Helena. "She is feeling very bad. She was very jealous of you. She was frightened too. She didn't want you to leave. She didn't want to be alone."

"Oh, poor Sharon!" says Treena. Now Treena feels very sad. "Why didn't Sharon tell me?"

"I don't know," says Helena. "But I think everything is OK now. Her friend Lisa has to leave her apartment. She will live with Sharon in your old apartment. She found the dress you bought her for the wedding. She likes it very much. She is excited to be your bridesmaid."

Stan comes back for the weekend and Treena and Stan go to see

Father Peter. On Sunday, Stan goes back to Manchester, and Treena goes back to her apartment. *Everything is wonderful now,* thinks Treena as she climbs the stairs. *My only worry is my dress!*

Sharon is waiting for her. She hugs Treena. "I am so sorry," says Sharon.

"I'm sorry too," says Treena. "I didn't understand your feelings."

"There's a surprise for you!" says Sharon.

She goes into the bedroom and Treena follows. The wedding dress is hanging on the door. It is wrapped up in a sheet.

Treena doesn't want to look at it. She remembers the red nail polish down the front of the skirt.

"Look at it!" says Sharon. Treena takes the dress and lays it on her bed. She unwraps the sheet.

"Oh!" she says.

The front of the dress is different. It is covered in lace. It is beautiful. The dress looks better than before.

"Helena took the dress away," says Sharon. "Her grandmother and her mother fixed the dress. The lace is from Poland. It is the lace from the grandmother's own wedding dress. Isn't it beautiful?"

"It's wonderful!" says Treena.

CHAPTER ELEVEN

It is November 15th. The church bells are ringing. Treena is walking into the church. Walking in front of her are Sharon, Karolina and Helena. Sharon and Helena found the red bridesmaid's dress on the Internet and bought two more.

Treena stops and looks around. The flowers from Gloria and her mother are beautiful. Her grandmother is sitting at the front of the church with the Kowalski family. The church is full of friends. Stan is waiting for her at the front of the church with his friends, Jaz and Culley.

He turns and smiles at her. The organ starts to play and Treena walks forward.

It is going to be the perfect wedding.

THANK YOU

Thank you for reading The Perfect Wedding. (Word count: 6,319) We hope you enjoyed it.

There are quizzes about this book on our free study site I Talk You Talk Press EXTRA. http://italk-youtalk.com

If you would like to read more graded readers, please visit our website http://www.italkyoutalk.com

Other Level 2 graded readers include
Adventure in Rome
Andre's Dream
A Passion for Music
Christmas Tales
Danger in Seattle
Don't Come Back
Finders Keepers…
Marcy's Bakery
Men's Konkatsu Tales
Salaryman Secrets!
Stories for Halloween
The House in the Forest
The School on Bolt Street
Train Travel
Trouble in Paris

Women's Konkatsu Tales

ABOUT THE AUTHOR

I Talk You Talk Press is a Japan-based publisher of language textbooks, graded readers and language learning/teaching resources.

Our team is made up of highly experienced language teachers and translators, who have all studied at least one additional language to an advanced level.

This experience enables us to design our materials from the perspective of both the teacher and the learner. We consult with both teachers and language learners when designing our textbooks and graded readers, and test our materials extensively in the classroom before publication.

We are a fast-growing press, and currently publish graded readers for learners of English. We publish new graded readers monthly.

www.ingramcontent.com/pod-product-compliance
Lightning Source LLC
Chambersburg PA
CBHW022351040426
42449CB00006B/818